The Science of Living Things

What is a Bat?

Bobbie Kalman & Heather Levigne

Crabtree Publishing Company
www.crabtreebooks.com

The Science of Living Things Series

A Bobbie Kalman Book

**For my parents, Mike and Marj Levigne
—there are no monsters at the end of this book!**

Editor-in-Chief
Bobbie Kalman

Writing team
Bobbie Kalman
Heather Levigne

Managing editor
Lynda Hale

Editors
April Fast
Kate Calder

Computer design
Lynda Hale

**Production coordinator
and photo researcher**
Hannelore Sotzek

Printer
Worzalla Publishing Company

Color separations and film
Dot 'n Line Image Inc.
CCS Princeton (cover)

Consultant
Barbara French, Conservation Information Specialist,
Bat Conservation International

Photographs
Russell C. Hansen: pages 8-9, 14-15
James Kamstra: page 17 (bottom)
Robert & Linda Mitchell: pages 12 (top), 16 (bottom), 18-19, 25 (bottom)
Photo Reasearchers, Inc.: Stephen Dalton: page 11; Nigel J. Dennis: page 29;
  Gilbert Grant: page 5; Stephen Krasemann: page 3; J.L. Lepore: page
  18 (inset); Merlin D. Tuttle, Bat Conservation International: front cover,
  title page, pages 8 (top), 9, 13, 17 (top), 26-27, 28
Roger Rageot/David Liebman Stock: pages 12 (bottom), 21, 24
James P. Rowan: page 25 (top)
Merlin D. Tuttle, Bat Conservation International: pages 4-5, 12 (middle),
  16 (top), 20 (both), 22, 23

Illustrations
Barbara Bedell: back cover, pages 4, 15
Cori Marvin: pages 6-7
Bonna Rouse: pages 5, 10, 30

Crabtree Publishing Company

www.crabtreebooks.com   1-800-387-7650

Cataloging in Publication Data
Kalman, Bobbie
   What is a bat?

(The science of living things)
Includes index.

ISBN 0-86505-883-0 (library bound)   ISBN 0-86505-895-4 (pbk.)
This book describes the main types of bats and discusses their physiology, feeding,
roosting, reproduction, echolocation abilities, and other behavior. 1. Bats—Juvenile lit-
erature. [1. Bats.] I. Levigne, Heather. II. Title. III. Series: Kalman, Bobbie.
Science of living things.
QL737.C5K25 1999   j579.4 21   LC 98-39285
                                                                 CIP

**Published in
the United States**
PMB 16A
350 Fifth Ave.
Suite 3308
New York, NY
10118

**Published
in Canada**
616 Welland Ave.,
St. Catharines,
Ontario, Canada
L2M 5V6

**Published in the
United Kingdom**
White Cross Mills
High Town, Lancaster
LA1 4XS
United Kingdom

**Published
in Australia**
386 Mt. Alexander Rd.,
Ascot Vale (Melbourne)
VIC 3032

Contents

What is a bat?

Bats are mammals. Mammals are warm-blooded, which means their body temperature stays the same in hot or cold weather. Like most mammals, bats are covered with fur and have a backbone. Female mammals carry their baby inside their body until birth. When the baby is born, it drinks milk from its mother's body. Bats are the only mammals that can fly. Most bats fly at night and rest during the day.

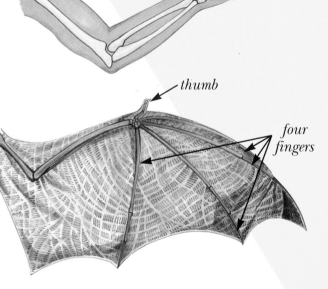

thumb

four fingers

The scientific name for bats is **chiroptera**, *which means hand-wing. Bat wings look like human hands.*

A flying fox can have a wing span up to five feet (1.5 meters) wide! Most flying foxes live in tropical areas of the world. Their huge wings help them travel long distances easily.

Difficult to study

Scientists are trying to learn more about bats, but bats can be difficult to catch and study. It takes a lot of patience to work with bats! During the day, most bats rest in places where they are well hidden from their enemies. At night, bats fly skillfully through the darkness. They can easily avoid objects in their path, including traps and nets.

Bats come in many sizes. This tiny banana bat is one of the smallest— it can fit in the palm of your hand.

When most animals hang upside down blood stays in their head. Bats have special valves in their veins that keep blood moving through their body when hanging.

Bat family tree

thumbless bat

There are almost a thousand **species**, or kinds, of bats. These species are divided into two groups—**megabats** and **microbats**. Megabats are large. Microbats are much smaller. Flying foxes and Old World fruit bats are the only two species of megabats. There are many species of microbats. Only two of the bats on these pages are megabats. Which are they?

New World disk-footed bat

mustached bat

horseshoe bat

Old World disk-footed bat

Bat ancestor

mammal with wings

shrewlike mammal

mammal with wing flaps

bat

Many scientists believe that the bat's closest relative is the shrew, a **nocturnal** mammal that feeds on insects.

Over millions of years, the small shrewlike mammals **evolved**, or slowly changed, to have wings.

free-tailed
bat

sheath-tailed bat

plain-nosed
bat

flying fox

Old World
leaf-nosed
bat

short-tailed
bat

mouse-tailed
bat

Old World
fruit bat

vampire bat

fishing
bat

slit-faced
bat

A bat's body

A bat's body is small and light. It is built for flying. Bats have large, strong wings to carry them through the air. Each bat's body is **adapted**, or suited, to the type of food it eats and the **habitat**, or place, in which it lives.

A bat has sharp claws on its feet to grip its **perch**, or resting place.

A bat's body is covered with fur. The bat uses its teeth, toenails, and tongue to **groom**; or clean, its fur.

Look at all the ridges and folds on this bat's ear! They help the bat hear sounds that a human cannot hear. Many bats rely on their hearing for hunting. Some bats have an extra flap of skin called a **tragus** on their ear. Scientists think the tragus helps bats hear quiet sounds such as an insect's footsteps.

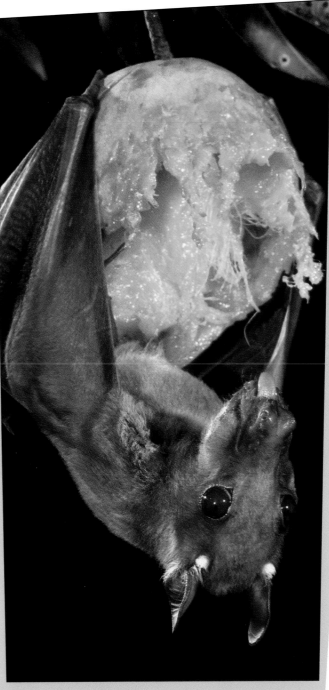

Bats use their wings...
- for flying
- to hold food when they eat
- to wrap around their body to keep themselves warm
- to fan their body to stay cool

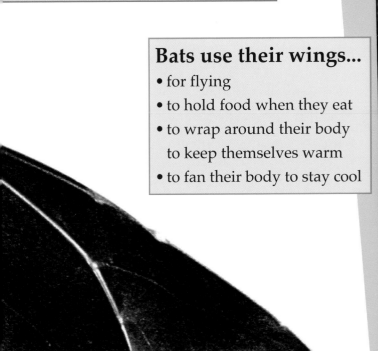

A bat's wings are made of thin, stretchy skin called **membrane**.

Bats that eat fruit have large eyes and good eyesight for finding food. Bats that hunt at night have small eyes. They use their sense of hearing to find food in the dark.

Echo-echo-echolocation

Echolocation is the way bats "locate" or find things. Instead of using their eyes, bats use echoes to find objects in the dark. All microbats and one species of megabat use echolocation.

How do they do that?

When a bat is using echolocation, it makes high-pitched sounds. The sounds bounce off objects in its path, creating echoes. The bat hears the echoes with its ears and can tell whether the object is a tree or something to eat. If the object is a tree, the bat turns to avoid hitting it. If it is food, the bat flies toward it.

Vviiiibrraaaatiiiiiions!

Touch your throat and speak. Do you feel your throat move? The tiny movements you feel are called **vibrations**. Your **larynx**, or voice box, vibrates when you make a sound. Microbats use their larynx to make sounds, too. Most microbats send sounds called **pulses** through their mouth. They fly with their mouth open to echolocate when they are hunting. Some microbats, such as the horseshoe bat, fly with their mouth closed. They have special **nose leafs** that they use to send out pulses.

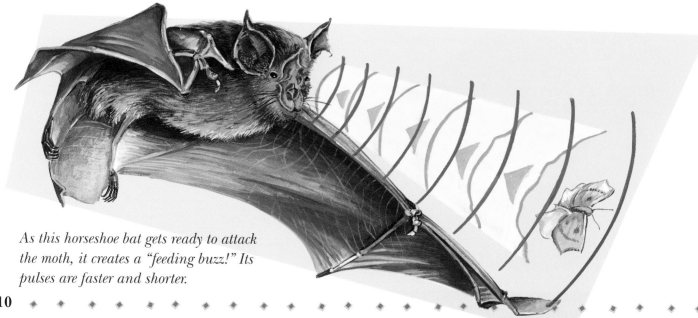

As this horseshoe bat gets ready to attack the moth, it creates a "feeding buzz!" Its pulses are faster and shorter.

Tongue-tied

Most megabats do not use echolocation, but the Egyptian fruit bat does. This bat lives in dark caves and needs echolocation to find its way in the dark. Unlike microbats, however, Egyptian fruit bats do not use their larynx to echolocate. They make sounds by clicking their tongue. You can make a similar sound by clicking your tongue against the roof of your mouth!

This fishing bat looks fierce with its teeth bared, but its mouth is open to send echolocation vibrations. Fishing bats use the long claws on their feet to snatch fish that they find swimming close to the water's surface.

Sight and smell

Like all other mammals, bats have five senses: taste, touch, hearing, sight, and smell. Bats use their senses of sight and smell to find food, select a mate, identify their baby, choose a **roost**, or resting place, and sense nearby predators.

The horseshoe bat's eyes are tiny. It uses echolocation instead of sight to find food.

Bats are not blind!

Many people believe that bats are blind, but all bats can see. Some have better eyesight than others, however. Megabats have large eyes. Their keen eyesight helps them find food in dim light. Microbats have small eyes, so they rely on echolocation to find food.

Fruit bats have a doglike face. They use their large eyes and nose to find food.

Smelling for food

What is your favorite food? How does it smell? Bats can smell their favorite foods, too. Some bats feed only on ripe fruit such as figs. These fruit-eating bats use their keen sense of smell to find the ripest, juiciest figs on the tree.

Vampire bats use their sense of smell to hunt large animals. Some vampire bats hunt together. When one bat sniffs out an animal on which to feed, the other bats gather to feed from the same animal.

The spear-shaped flap of skin on this bat's nose helps it find food.

The nose knows

Some bats are attracted to the scent of certain flowers. They drink flower **nectar**, or the sweet liquid inside flowers. Bats look for plants whose flowers open at night, such as the agave, India trumpet-flower, and baobab trees.

The Wahlberg's epauleted bat is heading toward a strong-smelling baobab blossom. The flower's light color and strong scent tell the bat there is a sweet treat inside!

On the wing

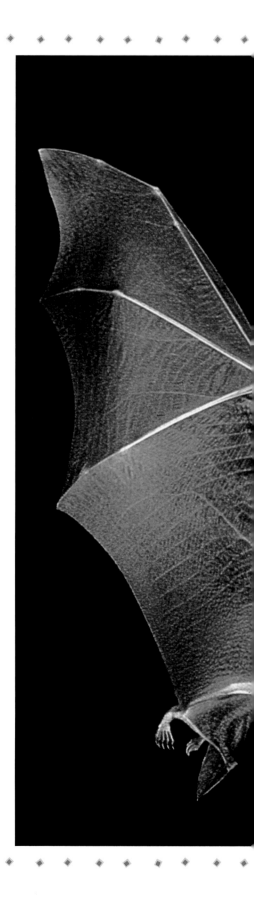

Flying helps bats find food and escape **predators**. Predators are animals that hunt and eat other animals to survive. Bats also fly to find good roosting sites and to **migrate**, or travel long distances when seasons change.

A bat's wings

Bat wings come in different shapes and sizes. Some bats have long, narrow wings, and others have short, broad wings. A bat's wing is made of thin membrane. Each wing has bones that make up the upper arm, forearm, four long fingers, and thumb. These bones are connected by membranes that the bat can fold in or stretch out. The membrane is attached to the sides of the bat's body and its hind legs.

Up, up, and away!

Bats use strong muscles in their shoulders, chest, and back to flap their wings and fly. They use one part of the wing for **lift** and another part for **thrust**. Lift keeps the bat up in the air. Thrust moves the bat forward. Bats flap their wings constantly to fly.

This photograph shows the two stages of a bat in flight. A bat raises its wings for lift and pushes them down to thrust itself through the air.

A bird's wing has feathers. A bat's wing has membrane. Although bats can fly, they cannot glide or soar the way a bird can. A bird's feathers are lighter than membrane. Air flows through spaces between them and allows the bird to glide.

Hanging out

Bats live all over the world, except in very hot or cold areas. Many species live in tropical areas such as West Africa. Others live in cooler areas such as North America. There may even be bats living in your backyard or attic!

Some bats, such as Spix's disk-winged bats, like to roost inside fresh green leaves. They lick the suction cups on their wrists and ankles to help them stick to the leaf's smooth surface.

When the sun goes down, millions of Mexican free-tailed bats rush from the cave's entrance to begin their nightly feeding.

A safe place to rest

A perch where bats rest or sleep is called a roost. Bats look for roosts that offer protection from danger and bad weather. Some like cool, dark roosts. Others prefer to roost in warm sunshine. Hanging upside down while roosting allows a bat to take flight quickly. It simply lets go and flies away!

*(right) Some megabats, such as Lyle's flying fox, roost in large groups called **camps**. Unlike most roosts, camps are in plain view. The bats are always on the lookout for predators.*

Hollows, *or gaps, in rock, wood, or plant material are perfect roosts for bats. Bats squeeze into small openings where they are safe from predators.*

Roosting habits

Bats have many different roosting habits. They may return to the same roost every night or look for a new roost. Some bats roost alone. Others, such as a mother bat and her baby, roost in pairs. Sometimes many bats roost together in a large cave. A large group of bats is called a **colony**. Vampire bats belong to the same colony their entire life.

Good night!

Some bats live in areas of the world that have long, cold winters. During the cold winter months, there are fewer plants and insects for bats to eat. Many bats **hibernate**, or sleep all winter. Some look for cool, dry roosts, such as buildings, in which to hibernate. Others choose burrows underground, where the air is warm and moist. Some bats hibernate alone, but others cluster together in large groups for warmth.

(inset) Many bats roost in a damp area while they are hibernating. Water has collected in droplets on this little brown bat's fur.

(right) These cave dawn bats are gathered on the ceiling of a cave in Indonesia.

Bat food

Bats need to eat food for **energy**. Energy is the physical power to do things. Flying uses a lot of energy, so bats need to eat large meals to replace the energy they use. Some bats eat up to 150 insects in only twenty minutes! Flying with a full stomach makes a bat too heavy, so a bat is able to digest its food quickly—often only twenty minutes after it has eaten.

Most bats eat insects such as moths, mosquitoes, and beetles. Some bats eat mainly fish. Fishing bats have large hind feet with long, sharp claws for spearing fish. After the bat catches a fish, it flies back to its roost to eat.

Fruit eaters

Many megabats eat soft, ripe fruit such as mangoes and bananas. They crush the fruit with their teeth and rub it against the roof of their mouth to squeeze out every bit of the pulp and juice. They spit out the tough fiber and seeds or pass it through their body as waste.

Some bats love the taste of nectar. They fly from flower to flower like a honeybee and use their long tongue to sip nectar from the bottom of each blossom.

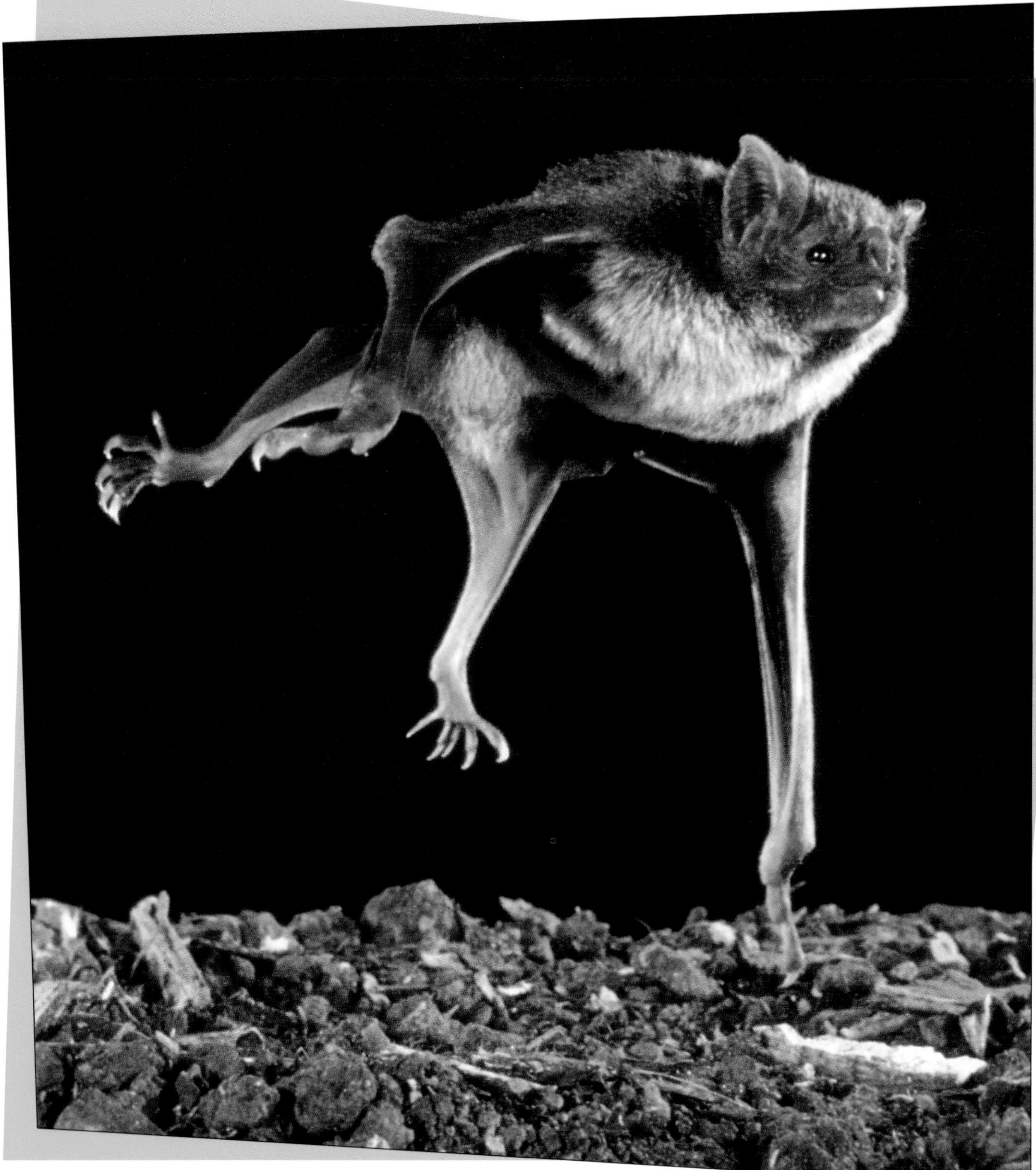

Vampire bats

Vampire bats are the only bats that drink blood. They feed on large mammals or farm animals such as cows and pigs. They land on the ground near their prey and walk around looking for a spot where the blood is close to the skin's surface. Using their sharp teeth, they make a small wound on the animal's skin. When the blood flows out of the wound, the bat laps it up with its tongue.

(opposite page) Vampire bats have stronger hind legs than those of most bats. They walk, run, and hop around their victim before sinking their fangs into the animal's flesh.

(below) Blood is harder to find than insects or fruit, so vampire bats share their meals with their roostmates.

Hey baby!

(above) Some bats carry their baby on their body until the baby learns to fly. Female bats have two false nipples. To hold onto their mother, the baby grasps a false nipple with its teeth. It also uses its thumbs and feet for holding on.

Baby bats are called **pups**. Most female bats have only one or two pups at once because they could not fly if they were carrying more babies. Bats give birth only when the weather is warm and there is a good supply of food. Bats that live in warm tropical areas where food is available all year round can have pups at any time of the year. Bats that live in places with cold winters have their young in the spring.

Giving birth

Most female bats give birth while they are hanging upside down, but some turn upright and hang by their thumbs. The mother bat catches her newborn using the skin between her hind legs. After they are born, baby bats begin **nursing**, or drinking milk, from their mother's **teats**, or real nipples.

Nurseries

Some pregnant female bats roost together in groups called **nursery colonies**. Some nursery colonies have as few as ten female bats, and others have more than a million. Bats form nurseries in warm places such as inside a cave or barn roof.

When the pups are born, the mother leaves them in the nursery while she searches for food. The pups cling to their roost while their mother is out looking for food. In large nurseries, they huddle together for warmth and protection. Sometimes they play, tumbling around while they wait for their supper. The mother bat and her baby make a special noise that helps them find each other when the mother bat returns.

Growing up

Most baby bats are born without fur. Their eyes are closed. A baby bat is very large when it is born. Its mouth and feet are almost the same size as those of an adult bat. Pups need a large mouth and strong feet to cling to their mother when she flies. Their wings, however, are small. As the pups grow, their wings get bigger and they learn how to fly.

Learning to fly

Most baby bats learn how to fly quickly. Little brown bats can fly eighteen days after they are born. Some, such as common vampire bats, may take as long as ten weeks before they are ready to fly. A mother bat may help her pup take its first flight, but the pup soon learns how to fly on its own. Once the pup can fly, it can begin to find its own food.

Under the watchful eye of its mother, this baby Gambian epauleted bat stretches its wings and learns how to fly.

Bats in nature

Did you know that bats help create new flowers and fruit trees? When a bat drinks nectar from a flower, **pollen** sticks to its fur. Pollen is the powdery material in the center of flowers. When the bat lands on another flower, some pollen rubs off onto that flower. Moving pollen from flower to flower is called **pollination**. Most plants cannot reproduce without pollination.

Passing seeds

Fruit-eating bats also help plants grow by dropping seeds in their body waste. After a bat eats, it flies back to its roost. Along the way, it digests its meal, passing seeds through its body. These seeds land on the ground and grow into new plants, flowers, and trees.

After this bat drinks the nectar from the flower, it will pollinate another flower with the pollen that has collected on its face.

Pest patrol!

Bats play an important role in nature. They are the natural enemies of many insects. Some bats can eat up to 600 insects in one hour! Bats get rid of many pests that ruin farmers' crops.

Loss of homes

Like all living things, bats need food and shelter to survive. When people cut down trees or disturb caves, many bats are left without a home. If a hibernating bat wakes up during the winter to fly away, it could use up all its energy and die.

Natural enemies

Snakes, hawks, mongooses, and weasels eat bats. Birds of prey and large bats catch other bats while they are flying. Some predators hunt where bats roost in colonies. When many bats fly out of their roost at once, a predator can quickly grab several bats out of the crowd.

The mongoose waits outside a cave and strikes when the bats fly out at dusk.

Bat chat

Many words begin or end with "bat." We used some of these words to make riddles about bats. Solve the riddles and write some of your own!

1. What do you call a bat on a trapeze?

2. Where do bats get their energy?

3. What did the bat use to make a cake?

5. Which lessons did the bat take?

4. Where did the bat have to go?

BATROOMS

BATMAN   BATWOMAN

Words to know

camps Large, noisy groups of megabats that roost together out in the open, such as in trees

colony A large group of bats that roosts together for warmth, protection, or reproduction

echolocation An animal's ability to locate objects in its environment by sending out and receiving sounds

energy The power needed to do things

evolve To change or develop slowly over time

habitat The natural place where a plant or animal lives

hibernate To sleep during the winter months

lift A force needed in flight for an object to rise into the air

mammal A warm-blooded animal that has a backbone

megabats Large bats

membrane A thin layer of tissue, or skin

microbats Small bats

migrate To move from one place to another when the seasons change

nocturnal Describing animals that are active at night

nose leaf A flap of skin on a bat's nose used to send pulses

nursery colony A large group of pregnant or nursing bats with their babies

pollinate To carry pollen fromone flower to another

predator An animal that is hunted and eaten by another animal

prey An animal that is hunted and eaten by anonther animal

pulses Sounds that bats make for echolocation

pups Baby bats

roost (n) The tree, cave, or building in which a bat rests; (v) to grip a perch by the feet

species A group of very similar living things whose offspring can make babies

thrust A force needed in flight to move forward through the air

tragus A small flap of skin on a bat's ear, which may be used for echolocation

warm-blooded Describing an animal whose body temperature stays the same regardless of the temperature of its environment

Index

0 Printed in the U.S.A. 7 6